Dragonflies
Water Angels and Brilliant Bioindicators

By Marta Magellan

Illustrated by Mauro Magellan

Eifrig Publishing LLC

Berlin Lemont

At Eifrig Publishing, our motto is our mission —
"Good for our kids, good for our Earth, and good for our communities."
We are passionate about helping kids develop into caring, creative, thoughtful
individuals who possess positive self-images, celebrate differences, and practice
inclusion. Our books promote social and environmental consciousness and
empower children as they grow in their communities.

www.eifrigpublishing.com

Published by Eifrig Publishing,
PO Box 66, Lemont, PA 16851, USA
Knobelsdorffstr. 44, 14059 Berlin, Germany.

For information regarding permission, write to:
Rights and Permissions Department,
Eifrig Publishing,
PO Box 66, Lemont, PA 16851, USA.
permissions@eifrigpublishing.com, +1-814-954-9445

Library of Congress Cataloging-in-Publication Data
Magellan, Marta
Anole Invasion/
by Marta Magellan, illustrated by Mauro Magellan,
Design by Rachel Magellan
p. cm.

Paperback: ISBN 978-1-63233-258-5
Hardcover: ISBN 978-1-63233-259-2
Ebook: ISBN 978-1-63233-260-8

[1. Nature – Juvenile Nonfiction. 2. Animals – Anoles, Lizards, Pollinators –
Juvenile Nonfiction
I. Magellan, Mauro, ill. II. Title

24 23 22 21 2020
5 4 3 2 1

Printed on recycled PCW acid-free paper. ∞

Dedications

In Loving Memory of Sammy Joe Schnall

To Sebastian Blake Schnall

- Marta

To Leah Estelle Magellan

- Mauro

Photo Credits

Giants of the Past

Long before dinosaurs roamed the earth, a huge insect zoomed over tropical forests. It looked like a giant version of dragonflies today. Except it had teeth! It clacked its huge wings, and gobbled up loads of bugs and even frogs. Sometimes called a griffinfly, it lived 100 million years before the dinosaurs took their first step.

Scientists who study ancient animals believe it was the largest insect of all time. Its wingspan was about the same as that of a hawk or eagle. Imagine one of those landing on your head! But you won't see any today. They became extinct with the arrival of flying reptiles.

Band-winged Dragonlet

Dragonflies Now

Today, dragonflies are not a bit scary. We like to think of them as water angels. Why? Let's follow two around and see. Don't worry about getting too close. Unlike wasps and spiders, dragonflies won't attack or sting you. Best of all, they don't carry disease like mosquitoes. In spite of the that fierce name, they're more like angels than dragons.

But what do they have to do with water?

Emperor Dragonfly

Hey, guys, over here! Clean water.

What Dragonflies Reveal

Fresh water is not as easy to come by as we think. We see it come out of our faucets as if it were free, and we take it for granted. Fresh water is precious.

It's a good sign to see a dragonfly. It means that nearby, there are healthy rivers, lakes, ponds, or marshes. If you see a waterway with no dragonflies, ever, it would be a bad sign. It would mean the water is **polluted** (unclean) and their eggs probably would not hatch. By being there, dragonflies reveal the good quality of the water. Scientists call them **bioindicators**.

What does that mean?

Needham's Skimmer

What is a Bioindicator?

Nobody really names wild insects, but let's call the dragonfly Ani because its scientific name is Anisoptera. Ani's cousin is the damselfly, Zygoptera. We'll call her Zygi. Imagine as we're following Ani around, we get lost and end up in a polluted waterway. Ani won't be there. Dragonflies don't hang out near water filled with **toxins**, chemicals that cause living things to get sick or die. That's what makes her such a good warning insect—a bioindicator.

Any animal can warn us about the cleanliness of their surroundings, but Ani is particularly good at it. Wherever dragonflies linger, we know the water is healthy for living things.

11

Female Dragonfly Laying Eggs

Ladies of the Water

Finally, Ani finds a sparkling lake. She zigs and zags back and forth up and down, across and around. She is searching for just the right spot to lay her eggs. Wherever she chooses to breed, it will always be either on, under, or at the water's edge. She might stop at a floating log or at some moss or mud along the shore. Or, she might find clumps of plants floating in shallow water. The most important thing is the purity of the water around the nest.

After much searching, she will land to deposit her eggs. The eggs hatch and live underwater until it is time to change into a dragonfly. The incredible transformation from egg to dragonfly is called **metamorphosis**.

METAMORPHOSIS
Dragonfly life cycle stages

Dragonfly Nymph

Immature Dragonflies

If Ani found good, clean water, the eggs hatch in a few weeks or in some species, a few months. Then, a little fish-like creature will shed its outer skin almost right away. Once the skin cracks, a six-legged **nymph** comes out. Underwater, the nymph breathes through gills. And this is unusual: Its gills are inside its butt.

That's no joke! The nymph breathes by inhaling water into its butt, and squeezing it back out again.

Adults would say it was being immature, but in this case, it's true—it's not an adult yet. But that's not all the nymph does that's kind of funny.

Adult Dragonfly Emerging from Nymph Shell

Speedy Nymphs

By squeezing water out of its butt, the dragonfly nymph can propel itself in the opposite direction, rocketing forward like a jet ski. It is speedy enough to chase minnows and tadpoles for breakfast. It feeds on immature mosquito **larvae**, too (yay!). The nymph will live one to four years underwater. Its skin will **molt** (shed) about twelve times. Finally, the skin dries out, and the old nymph shell will split open so that an adult dragonfly can emerge.

Eastern Pondhawk

Lords and Ladies of the Air

Following Ani around isn't easy. Dragonflies are remarkable flyers. Some species travel thousands of miles, even over oceans, perfectly at home over large bodies of water. They take to the air vertically and hover like a helicopter for minutes at a time. Not only can they fly forwards, but they can go backwards, too. And they are capable of making surprising zig-zag twists and turns through the reeds. What gives them this amazing ability? The dragonfly's front and back wings are not connected to each other and can beat separately. They can chase a lot of mosquitoes with those wings.

Dragonfly Eyes

Perfect Hunting Eyes

If we pick up a magnifying glass and look at Ani's eyes, we'll see compound eyes with thousands of parts. Eyes like these help both Ani and Zygi have great eyesight. They can detect insects (their **prey**) to the left and right, above and below them. Zygi's eyes are wide apart, while Ani's touch each other.

Ani and Zygi are perfect hunting machines. If you watch Ani closely, you'll see that with only a tiny turn of her head, she can even see what's behind her. She will perch and wait until she sees a small insect flying overhead. Then she darts toward the prey and captures it from underneath.

Damselfly with Prey

Handy Hunting Legs

When we think of legs, we usually think of walking. But neither Ani nor Zygi can walk like other animals.

Would you like flies with that?

Instead, their legs are made to catch flying insects while dashing through the air. Their legs point forward, so they can grab their prey on the fly. Both Ani and Zygi make a kind of basket with their legs and scoop their prey with them. If the prey is too big, they will perch somewhere to eat it. But Ani can easily eat her basket of mosquitoes in mid-flight. That's what we call fast food!

Needham's Skimmer

How They Got Their Name

Why call them dragonflies when they look nothing like dragons? Strangely enough, both Native American and European folk stories claim they were once dragons. Actually, people have called them all kinds of names. Old Floridians called them mosquito hawks because they ate so many of those pesky critters. Dragonflies were often called water witches, devil's horse or devil's needle.

Luckily, the name dragonfly stuck—it's an awesome name for an awesome insect.

Great Pondhawk

Angels or Devils?

In Europe, there is a myth that dragonflies will poke out people's eyes or sew up their mouths. Old Swedish folktales claim that when a dragonfly hovers around you, it is weighing your soul for the devil. Unlike those creepy myths, the medicine men and women of the Pueblo tribes in the southwestern United States thought better of dragonflies. They believed the dragonfly's spirit healed people. And when dragonflies appeared near water, the Navajos believed the water was pure enough to drink (how true). Although some people nicknamed them water witches, we know now they're more like water angels. We need them to survive and be bioindicators. They will keep us informed about the quality of our Earth's scarce and precious fresh water.

WORLD'S WATER INFOGRAPHIC

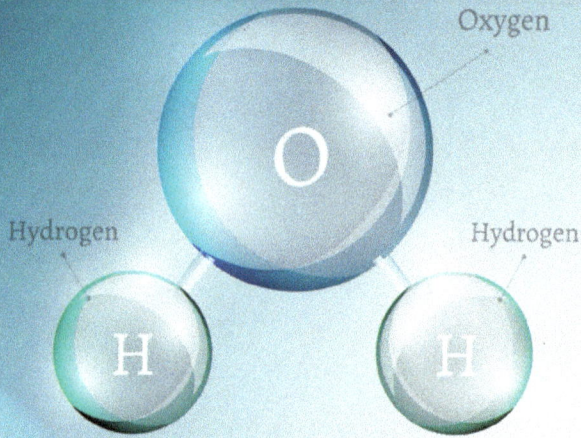

Oxygen

O

Hydrogen

H

Hydrogen

H

Water - H2O

Water is the driving force *of all nature.*

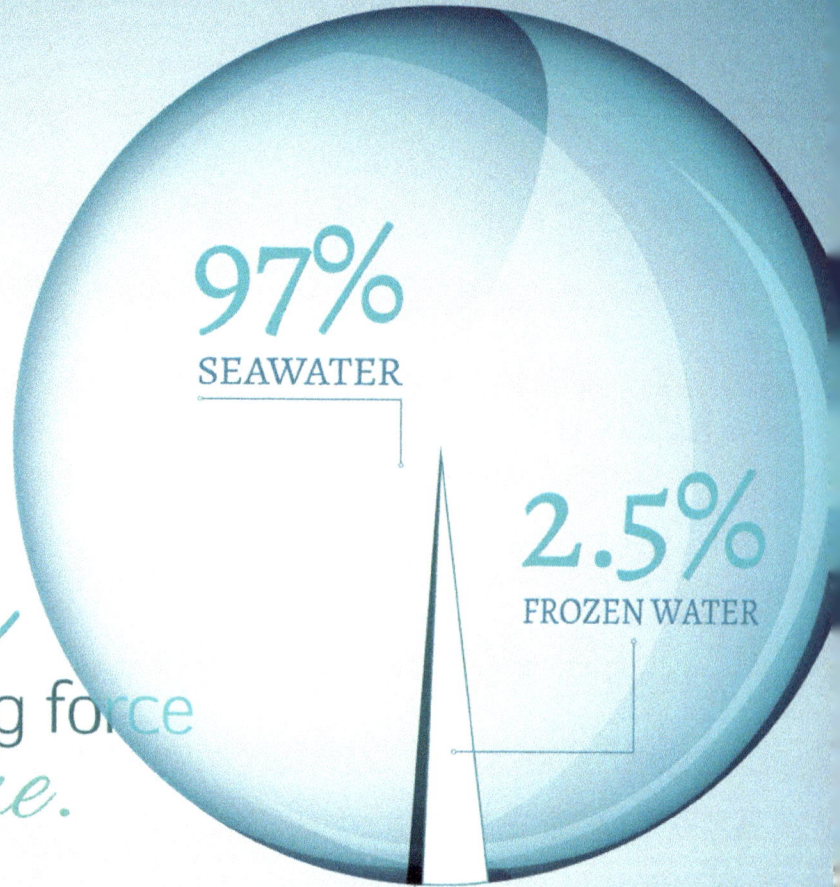

97%
SEAWATER

2.5%
FROZEN WATER

0.5%
FRESH WATER

Precious Water

We think it's unlimited, we waste it, and we even pay too much to drink it from little plastic bottles. Water. The earth has more ocean than land, but most of it, around 97% is saltwater. Only about one half to 1 percent of all freshwater is accessible in rivers, lakes and streams. The rest of it is stuck deep underground and in glaciers.

Water needs to be conserved.

What You Can Do at Home

1. Turn Off the Faucet

While brushing your teeth or soaping your hands and face, turn off the faucet to keep water from running down the drain.

2. Tightly Turn the Faucet so that There are No Drips.

Drips can waste a lot of water over time. If there is a leak, tell your parents about it. Leaks should be fixed and drips stopped.

3. Shower Instead of Bathe

When you are old enough, switch from baths to quick showers. They use less water than filling up a tub.

4. Watering Plants

In places where it rains enough, tell your parents about collecting rain water in barrels to water plants and grass.

5. Avoid Bottled Water

Companies take water from springs or even from faucets like yours and pour it into plastic bottles. That water costs a lot of money and the plastic is a disaster for the oceans. You can filter your own tap water with a filtering jug.

6. Choose Native Plants

By planting trees and plants for your yard that do not need excessive watering, you will be supporting native wildlife and conserving water, too—a double win.

29

➤ More Facts About Dragonflies

- The giant ancient insect resembling a dragonfly, Meganeura monyi, lived during the Carboniferous period. Meganeuropsis lived during the Permian period of the Palaeozoic era (300 million years ago).

- Dragonflies inhabit every part of the world except the frozen Antarctic.

- There are more than 5,000 known species of dragonflies.

- Both dragonflies and damselflies belong to the order Odonata.

- Florida alone has over 100 species of dragonflies.

- Dragonflies are capable of longer, more robust flights, while damselflies have weak, fluttery flight. It's easy to tell them apart. When they perch, dragonflies keep their wings spread out, while damselflies keep theirs closed along their abdomens.

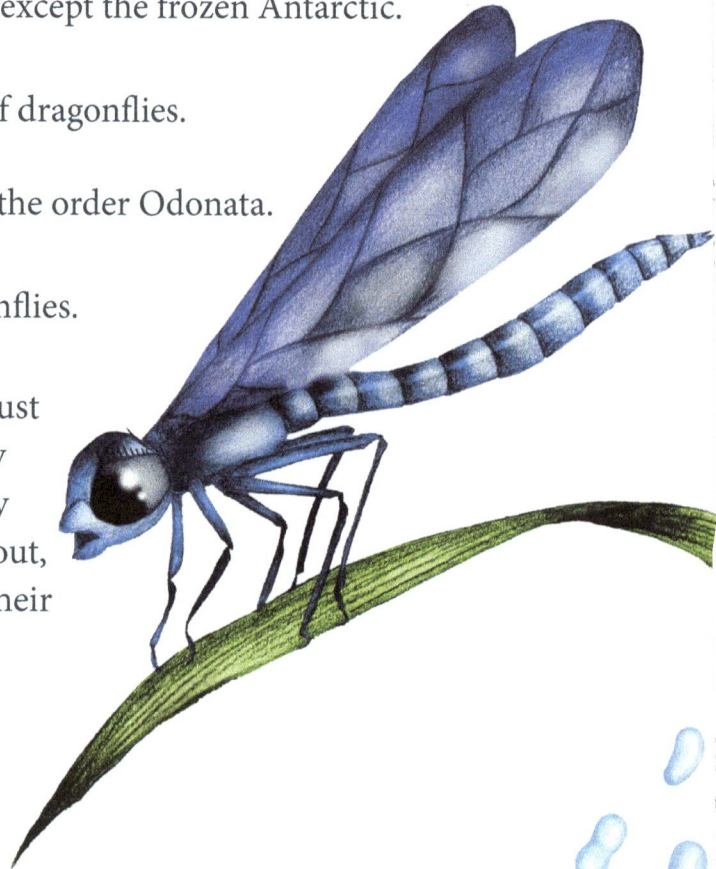

Glossary

Anisoptera: A group of insects which consists of the dragonflies.

Bioindicator: A living organism that gives us an indication (idea) of the health of an ecosystem.

Damselfly: Also of the Odonata order, but more slender and with weaker flight abilities.

Ecosystem: An ecosystem is made up of all of the living and nonliving things in an area, such as animals, plants, water, rocks, and sand.

Habitat: A habitat is the area where an animal or plant lives. Most habitats include a community of animals and plants along with water, climate, soil, and sand. Planet Earth has many different habitats where animals and plants live, from dry deserts to lush tropical forests. With only a few exceptions, dragonflies develop in water, so some type of water habitat is necessary for their breeding and survival.

Larva, Larvae (plural): A young wingless form of many animals, notably insects that hatch from eggs.

Metamorphosis: The process of an insect or amphibian changing from an immature stage to a full-grown adult, like butterflies and dragonflies.

Molt: When an animal sheds old skin or an old shell to make way for new growth.

Myth: A popular belief or traditional story that is not true, but is used to explain natural phenomenon or anything that is not understood or known.

Nymph: Also called larva, a nymph is the young form of many insects. In the case of dragonflies, nymphs live in water for as long as four or five years before becoming adults and taking to the air.

Odonata: The order of insects that comprises both the dragonflies and damselflies. They have long, slender bodies, two pairs of wings, large compound eyes, and larvae that lives in water.

Polluted: Dirty, foul, contaminated—in this book as it applies to water.

Prey: Animals hunted and eaten by other animals.

Predator: An animal who hunts and eats other animals.

Unpolluted: Not dirty, contaminated or polluted.

Zygoptera: A group of insects which covers the damselflies.

Acknowledgements

Many thanks to Professor Emeritus Chris Migliaccio of Miami Dade College, environmental science, biology, and ecology expert, who edited the manuscript.

A special thank-you goes to Cathy Snyder and her passion for the Nature Detectives and for her boundless hospitality. Thank you also goes to publisher Penny Eifrig for her belief in the importance of sustainability. Without their help and encouragement, this book would not have been possible.

I am also grateful to Anne Crawford, Youth Services Coordinator, St. John's County Public Library System, Marcia Daniels, whose knowledge of dragonflies helped with the content included in the book, Marilyn Smith, of the Sisterhood of the Traveling Plants, and all the members of the St. Augustine Garden Club for supporting reading and learning through the Nature Detectives workshops.

My niece, Rachel Magellan, and brother, Mauro Magellan, whose generous help with design and illustration has made this book an enjoyable family project.

And of course, Silvia Lopez, all the members of the Coral Gables critique group and the members of the West Dade Regional writing group who reviewed this manuscript: Nydia Busch, Liza Flores-Garcia, Cristina Keller, Donna Kurtz, Paul Kurtz, Aixa Perez-Padro, and Karen Marleen Strangwayes.

My deep gratitude to the source of my greatest happiness: my daughter, Tracy Monique, and her family, Jeremy, Sammy, and Sebastian, my son Marc Gabriel, and husband James.

www.ingramcontent.com/pod-product-compliance
Lightning Source LLC
Chambersburg PA
CBHW060753150426

42811CB00058B/1394